Cooking
for Kids

Cooking for Kids

Bounty
Books

First published in Great Britain in 1999 by
Hamlyn, a division of Octopus Publishing
Group Ltd

This edition published in 2007 by Bounty Books, a
division of Octopus Publishing Group Ltd
2–4 Heron Quays, London E14 4JP

An Hachette Livre UK Company

ISBN: 978-0-753716-28-1

A CIP catalogue record for this book is available
from the British Library

Printed and bound in China

Notes

1 Standard level spoon measurements are
used in all recipes.

1 tablespoon = one 15 ml spoon
1 teaspoon = one 5 ml spoon

2 Both imperial and metric measurements
have been given in all recipes. Use one set of
measurements only and not a mixture of both.

3 Measurements for canned foods have been
given as a standard metric equivalent.

4 Eggs should be medium unless otherwise
stated. The Department of Health advises that
eggs should not be consumed raw. This book
may contain dishes made with lightly cooked
eggs. It is prudent for more vulnerable people,
such as pregnant and nursing mothers,
invalids, the elderly, babies and young
children, to avoid uncooked or lightly cooked
dishes made with eggs. Once prepared, these
dishes should be used immediately.

5 Milk should be full fat unless otherwise
stated.

6 Poultry should always be cooked
thoroughly. To test if poultry is cooked, pierce
the flesh through the thickest part with a
skewer or fork – the juices should run clear,
never pink or red.

7 Fresh herbs should be used unless
otherwise stated. If unavailable, use dried
herbs as an alternative but halve the
quantities stated.

8 Pepper should be freshly ground black
pepper unless otherwise stated; season
according to taste.

9 Ovens should be preheated to the specified
temperature – if using a fan-assisted oven,
follow the manufacturer's instructions for
adjusting the time and the temperature.

10 Do not re-freeze a dish that has been
frozen previously.

11 This book includes dishes made with nuts
and nut derivatives. It is advisable for
customers with known allergic reactions to
nuts and nut derivatives and those who may
be potentially vulnerable to these allergies,
such as pregnant and nursing mothers,
invalids, the elderly, babies and young
children, to avoid dishes made with nuts and
nut oils. It is also prudent to check the labels
of pre-prepared ingredients for the possible
inclusion of nut derivatives.

12 Vegetarians should look for the 'V' symbol
on a cheese to ensure it is made with
vegetarian rennet. There are vegetarian forms
of Parmesan, feta, Cheddar, Cheshire, red
Leicester, dolcelatte and many goats' cheeses,
among others.

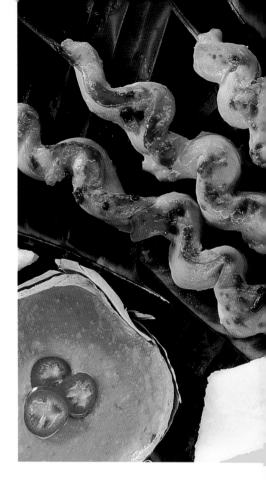

introduction 6

light bites
& snacks 10

Great recipes for after school snacks
and quick and simple in-between
meals to satisfy growing eaters.
Children can even help prepare some
of the easier recipes such as salads
and sandwiches.

surf & turf 30

A little imagination can make all the
difference in making mealtimes for
kids fun. Here you will find a balanced
selection of healthy meals with classic
favourites like kebabs and burgers.

pasta & pizza 52

Pasta is an great cupboard ingredient
and works well with many fresh
flavours. Pizza is a great food for kids
as they can personalize a basic recipe
with the toppings of their choice.

yummy treats 66

Not just for little eaters! This mouth
watering selection of desserts and
puddings will be sure to put a smile on
the face of little and big kids alike.

mocktails 86

Making shakes and punches is an easy
yet special means of getting kids to
drink milk and healthy fruit juices.
Many of the recipes would be fun for a
kids party as well.

index 96

contents

introduction

Cooking for kids can be a challenging experience. Children can be unwilling to try new flavours, and may be more enthusiastic about junk food than meals that you consider to be healthy and nutritionally balanced. However, with a little ingenuity, you can compete with peer group pressure and the attractively packaged junk food that they like so much. Food should be fun and if you present it in an appealing way and encourage children to help when you are cooking, they will want to eat what they have made – and you can decide on the ingredients used. Start off as you mean to go on when children are young and offer a wide range of foods to ensure a good balance of nutrients and to allow your child to try new flavours and textures. If you establish an enjoyment of cooking early and encourage healthy eating habits, it will stand children in good stead for adult life.

Well balanced
A well-balanced diet means offering children a mixture of foods with the right amount of calories to provide energy, as well as all the necessary nutrients for growth and health.

To help you plan daily meals, foods are divided into various groups. Serve generous amounts each day from the following two groups:

Cereals and grains
This includes bread, pasta, rice and oats. These foods provide the vital energy that growing children need and also contain essential vitamins and minerals. Wholegrain cereals and bread contain fibre although it is best to introduce this gradually as children may not be able to cope with too much roughage. Starchy foods such as potatoes are also high in energy and can be served baked, steamed, boiled or mashed.

Vegetables and fruit
These contain vitamin C, essential for growth, healthy bones, teeth and gums, healing of wounds and absorption of iron, and vitamin A, for healthy skin and eyes. Vegetables and fruit are best served raw or lightly cooked. Use frozen food only as a standby and avoid canned fruit in sugar syrup and canned vegetables in salt. If you use canned beans, such as red kidney beans, rinse them well in water and drain before using. Include at least two helpings of fresh vegetables each day and four helpings of fruit. If you find it difficult to get your child to eat vegetables, you can use them in blended soups or add to favourite dishes such as lasagne or spaghetti bolognaise. Most children enjoy homemade fruit or vegetable drinks made in a liquidizer or food processor and you can add milk or yogurt for extra nutrition. Dress them up with fun fruit or vegetable shapes and serve them with bright, bendy straws.

'They dined on mince, and slices of quince,

Which they ate with a runcible spoon;

And hand in hand, on the edge of the sand,

They danced by the light of the moon.'

Edward Lear *The Owl and the Pussy Cat*

Serve smaller amounts each day from the following two groups:

Meat and other protein foods
This group provides protein which is vital for healthy growth, as well as vitamins and minerals. It includes poultry, white fish and oily fish, eggs, nuts (ground rather than whole), lentils, beans and peas. Choose white meats and fish rather than red meats and select only lean cuts of meat with no visible fat.

Dairy foods
These include milk, cheese and yogurt and provide an adequate intake of calcium and phosphorus, necessary for healthy bones and teeth. Choose full-fat milk until your child is at least two years old, then change to semi-skimmed if you are sure that all energy needs are adequately supplied. Offer a selection of mild hard cheeses, cottage cheese or pasteurized full-fat yogurt. Fresh fruit can be added to unsweetened yogurt.

Limit foods from these two groups:

Fats and oils
Although children do need some fat in their diet for energy, it is best not to eat too much saturated fat, which is found in animal sources. Any excess fat eaten is stored in the body as fat. Choose lean meat, and spread butter or margarine thinly on bread. Use healthy cooking methods such as poaching, steaming, grilling or baking, rather than frying.

Sugar, and foods and drinks containing sugar
These foods are not essential for a balanced diet and provide only calories without any nutritional value and so should be limited to the occasional treat. They also diminish the appetite for healthier food. Encourage your child to eat fresh fruit, raisins or dates as a snack instead of biscuits or sweets. Make fruit shakes and smoothies and serve them in attractive containers to tempt your child. Many processed foods contain sugars, so serve fresh food whenever possible.

Meal appeal
Junk food is always popular with kids, but the high salt and fat content can be very unhealthy if it is eaten regularly. Substitute your own homemade burgers and baked oven chips, when you can control the ingredients used, and add flavour with herbs and mild spices. Serve small portions because too much food on a plate can be off-putting. Add small amounts of vegetables so you can see which your child prefers. If cooked vegetables are a problem, offer them raw or add them to a lightly cooked stir-fry. Colour and texture make a meal more attractive, and you can arrange fruit and vegetables in patterns or make pizzas or sandwiches with faces. Don't add too many flavours at once, and serve different foods separately so that your child can make a choice. If your child likes food mixed up, make casseroles and risottos with added vegetables.

Kids in the kitchen
Most kids love helping in the kitchen and will happily make shapes with pastry, cut out shapes for biscuits or make patterns from pasta shapes. Start off by giving them simple tasks such as weighing out ingredients or washing vegetables, then get them to make something more interesting, such as mini jam tarts. Popcorn is another fun thing to make, but keep your eye on the hot pan or make it in a microwave. Don't worry too much about the mess kids make while learning to cook, it's worth it if they are to enjoy cooking.

Safety first
When your children help you in the kitchen it is a good opportunity to teach them about safety so that accidents can be avoided. The obvious dangers are hot liquids, hot ovens and hotplates and electrical equipment. Show your child how to handle these or impress on him or her not to do anything unless you are there to super-vise. Make sure they wash their hands before handling food and to leave everything clean and tidy when they have finished.

cheesy waffles •

potato cakes & mushroom sauce •

mini bacon & sausage rolls •

sandy courgette fritters •

cucumber & strawberry salad •

cheese scones •

nutty orange flapjacks •

hot apple muffins •

appletree salad •

toasted traffic lights •

parmesan cheese twists •

tuna scramble rolls •

corn chowder •

sunshine citrus croissants •

pick up potatoes with creamy dip •

light bites & snacks

cheesy waffles

1 Sift the flour, baking powder and salt into a bowl and add the oat flakes. Beat the eggs, butter and milk in another bowl. Make a well in the centre of the flour and pour in half the egg mixture. Beat well together and gradually beat in the remaining liquid to form a light batter. Prepare a waffle iron and cook until the waffles are golden brown on both sides.

2 To make the topping, put all the ingredients into a bowl and lightly mix together.

3 To serve, place a spoonful of the cheese topping on each waffle and garnish with a sprig of dill.

125 g (4 oz) wholemeal flour

2 teaspoons baking powder

pinch of salt

50 g (2 oz) fine oat flakes

2 eggs, separated

50 g (2 oz) butter

300 ml (½) pint milk

Topping:

250 g (8 oz) ricotta cheese

2 tablespoons sunflower seeds

1 tablespoon sesame seeds

4 tomatoes, skinned and chopped

4 spring onions, chopped

sprigs of dill, to garnish

Makes 10
Preparation time: 15 minutes
Cooking time: about 25 minutes

potato cakes & mushroom sauce

1 Grate the potatoes very finely and squeeze out excess liquid. Place in a bowl and stir in the onion, dill, salt and flour. Stir the egg into the potato mixture until evenly combined.

2 Heat 1 cm (½ inch) oil in a large nonstick frying pan. Divide the potato mixture into 8 cakes and fry in batches, pressing the cakes flat, for 3–4 minutes on each side until golden. Drain the potato cakes on kitchen paper and keep warm.

3 To make the sauce, gently melt the butter in a pan and fry the shallots and garlic for 5 minutes. Add the mushrooms and stir-fry over a moderate heat for 5–6 minutes until golden and tender.

4 Remove from the heat and stir in the dill, soured cream, horseradish. Serve the potato cakes topped with some mushroom sauce and dill sprigs.

375 g (12 oz) waxy potatoes

½ small onion, very thinly sliced

1 tablespoon chopped dill

½ teaspoon salt

15 g (½ oz) self-raising flour

1 egg, beaten

vegetable oil, for frying

Mushroom Sauce:

25 g (1 oz) butter

2 shallots, chopped

1 garlic clove, crushed

375 g (12 oz) button mushrooms

2 tablespoons chopped dill

6 tablespoons soured cream

2 teaspoons creamed horseradish

dill sprigs, to garnish

Serves 4
Preparation time: 20 minutes
Cooking time: 25–30 minutes

mini bacon & sausage rolls

1 Stretch the bacon rashers with the back of a knife. Wind one rasher along the length of each sausage and fasten with a wooden cocktail stick.

2 Arrange the sausage parcels on a grill rack and cook under a preheated moderate grill for about 7–8 minutes on each side.

16 rashers of streaky bacon, rinded

16 pork chipolata sausages

Makes 16
Preparation time: 5 minutes
Cooking time: about 15 minutes

sandy courgette fritters

1 First make the dip. Place all the ingredients in a small bowl and stir well until evenly combined. Set aside for 30 minutes for the flavours to infuse.

2 Cut the courgettes into thin slices about 5 mm (¼ inch) thick. Mix the polenta and flour in a large bowl and season lightly with salt and pepper. Dip the courgettes into the egg and then into the polenta to coat evenly and thoroughly.

3 Put about 10 cm (4 inches) of oil into a large, deep saucepan and heat to 180°–190°C (350°–375°F), or until a cube of bread browns in 30 seconds. Fry the courgette slices in batches for 2–3 minutes until crisp and golden. Drain on kitchen paper and serve hot with the dip.

500 g (1 lb) courgettes
25 g (1 oz) polenta
25 g (1 oz) plain flour
1 egg, lightly beaten
vegetable oil, for deep frying
salt and pepper

Cool Dunking Dip:
125 g (4 oz) natural yogurt
1 garlic clove, crushed
1 tablespoon chopped mint
125 g (4 oz) cucumber, peeled, grated and squeezed dry

Serves 6–8
Preparation time: 20 minutes plus infusing
Cooking time: 8–12 minutes

■ Polenta is a type of coarse flour made from cornmeal. If you can't find polenta, you could use semolina instead.

cucumber & strawberry salad

1 Place the cucumber slices in a bowl. Add the oil and vinegar, and pepper to taste. Toss lightly.

2 Arrange the cucumber and strawberry slices on a serving platter or individual plates. Scatter a few mint leaves on top. Chill for at least 30 minutes before serving.

1 small cucumber, peeled and very thinly sliced

1 tablespoon grapeseed oil or light olive oil

1 teaspoon white wine vinegar

250 g (8 oz) strawberries, hulled and thinly sliced

pepper

mint leaves, to decorate

Serves 4

Preparation time: 15 minutes plus chilling

cheese scones

1 Sift the flour, salt, mustard and baking powder into a mixing bowl. Cut the fat into the flour and rub it in with the fingertips until the mixture resembles fine breadcrumbs. Mix in the grated cheese. Beat the egg with half of the liquid and stir into the dry ingredients. Work into a soft dough adding more liquid as necessary.

2 Turn on to a well-floured board and roll out lightly until 1.5 cm (¾ inch) thick. Cut out rounds with a 6.5 cm (2¾ inch) cutter. Gather the remaining dough together, roll again and cut more rounds. Place all the rounds on a warmed baking sheet. Brush with milk and sprinkle with grated cheese.

3 Bake in a preheated oven, 220°C (425°F) Gas Mark 7, for 10–15 minutes until well risen and golden. Cool on a wire rack. Serve with butter, cream cheese and cherry tomatoes or a salad filling.

250 g (8 oz) plain flour

½ teaspoon salt

1 teaspoon dry mustard

4 teaspoons baking powder

50 g (2 oz) butter or margarine

75–125 g (3–4 oz) mature Cheddar cheese, grated

1 egg, beaten

150 ml (¼ pint) milk or water

milk, for brushing

grated cheese, for sprinkling

Makes about 12
Preparation time: 15 minutes
Cooking time: 10–15 minutes

nutty orange flapjacks

1 Grease an 18 cm (7 inch) square shallow tin.

2 Heat the butter, sugar and honey in a medium saucepan over low heat, stirring with a wooden spoon until the ingredients have melted together. Remove the pan from the heat. Stir in the oats, nuts and orange rind. Mix well and spoon into the tin, pressing down lightly.

3 Bake the mixture in a preheated oven, 180°C (350°F) Gas Mark 4, for 25 minutes. Leave to cool, easing the cake away from the sides of the tin with a sharp knife. When the cake is cool, cut into bars.

125 g (4 oz) butter

50 g (2 oz) demerara sugar

2 tablespoons clear honey

175 g (6 oz) rolled oats

25 g (1 oz) chopped nuts

finely grated rind of 1 orange

Makes 12 bars

Preparation time: 5 minutes

Cooking time: 25 minutes

1 Grease 24 x 5 cm (2 inch) muffin or bun tins. Sift the flour, salt and baking powder into a mixing bowl. Stir in the sugar and spices. In a small bowl beat the eggs with the milk and mix in the melted butter. Stir the liquid quickly into the flour mixture. Speed is essential once the liquid is added to the baking powder, so do not beat the mixture or bother about any lumps. Fold in the chopped apples. Spoon the mixture into the greased muffin or bun tins so they are one-third full.

2 Bake in a preheated oven, 190°C (375°F) Gas Mark 5, for 15–20 minutes or until well risen and golden brown. Turn out of the tins and serve hot, split and buttered.

250 g (8 oz) plain flour

1 teaspoon salt

3 teaspoons baking powder

50 g (2 oz) caster sugar

½ teaspoon ground ginger

½ teaspoon mixed spice

2 eggs, beaten

150 ml (¼ pint) milk

50 g (2 oz) butter, melted

250 g (8 oz) cooking or dessert apples, peeled, cored and finely chopped

Makes 24

Preparation time: 15 minutes

Cooking time: 15–20 minutes

hot apple muffins

appletree salad

1 Mix all the dressing ingredients together until well blended. Toss the apple slices in the lemon juice. Mix together the apple and mushroom slices, the grapes, carrots and celery. Sprinkle with the sesame seeds.

2 Pour on the dressing and mix well to serve. Alternatively, serve the dressing separately.

Lemon juice prevents the apple slices from turning brown, and also adds a tangy flavour to this healthy salad.

2 red eating apples, cored and thinly sliced

2 teaspoons lemon juice

125 g (4 oz) mushrooms, thinly sliced

250 g (8 oz) red grapes, halved and seeded

2 carrots, grated

2 celery sticks, sliced

2 tablespoons roasted sesame seeds

Dressing:

2 tablespoons olive oil

1 tablespoon apple juice

2 tablespoons soured cream

salt and pepper

Serves 4–6

Preparation time: 20 minutes

toasted traffic lights

1 Cut each slice of bread into a rectangle about 10 x 6.5 cm (4 x 2½ inches).

2 Toast half the bread slices on 1 side only. Then spread the untoasted sides with cream cheese.

3 Using a 2.5 cm (1 inch) round cutter, stamp out 3 rounds from the remaining slices, then place on the top of the cream cheese.

4 Spoon the strawberry, apricot and greengage jams into the holes, to resemble traffic lights. Toast quickly until lightly browned. Cool slightly before serving.

8 slices white or brown bread

1 tablespoon strawberry or raspberry jam

1 tablespoon apricot jam

75 g (3 oz) cream cheese

1 tablespoon greengage jam

Serves 4

Preparation time: 10 minutes

---

1 Roll the pastry on a clean, lightly floured work surface to a rectangle 30 x 25 cm (12 x 10 inches). Spread with the mustard or marmite and sprinkle over the cheese. Fold in half and roll lightly.

2 Cut the pastry into about 20 long, thin strips. Sprinkle half with poppy seeds and the other half with sesame seeds. Twist the strips and arrange on baking sheets. Bake in a preheated oven, 190°C (375°F) Gas Mark 5, for about 15 minutes or until puffy and golden.

500 g (1 lb) puff pastry

2 tablespoons coarse-grain mustard or marmite

50 g (2 oz) Parmesan cheese, grated

1 tablespoon poppy seeds

1 tablespoon sesame seeds

Makes about 20
Preparation time: 15 minutes
Cooking time: 15 minutes

parmesan cheese twists

■ Puff pastry is a rich, multi-layered crisp pastry which is complicated to make. However, the ready-made versions are really just as good to use.

1 Mash the tuna in a bowl with the lemon juice and season to taste with pepper. Stir in the parsley.

2 Beat the eggs in a bowl. Melt half the butter in a small saucepan, add the egg mixture and stir over a gentle heat for about 5 minutes until the eggs are set but still creamy. Remove from the heat and set aside to cool. Split the rolls and spread the halves with the remaining butter.

3 Spread the tuna mixture over the bottom half of each roll. Spoon on the scrambled egg and cover with the top halves of the rolls.

200 g (7 oz) can tuna, drained

1 tablespoon lemon juice

1 tablespoon chopped parsley

4 eggs

50 g (2 oz) butter, softened

4 granary rolls

pepper

Makes 4
Preparation time: 10 minutes
Cooking time: 5 minutes

tuna scramble rolls

corn chowder

1 Melt the butter in a medium saucepan over a moderate heat. Cook the onion and pepper for about 4–5 minutes until soft but not brown. Stir in the flour and cook for 1 minute. Add the stock gradually, stirring continuously. Still stirring, add the milk and bring to the boil.

2 Add the potatoes to the pan with the mushrooms and sweet-corn. Season to taste. Reduce the heat and simmer gently for 20–25 minutes until the potatoes are tender, stirring occasionally. Sprinkle with the chives before serving.

25 g (1 oz) butter

1 medium onion, chopped

1 small green or red pepper, cored, deseeded and chopped

25 g (1 oz) plain flour

450 ml (¾ pint) chicken or vegetable stock

450 ml (¾ pint) skimmed milk

2 medium potatoes, diced

125 g (4 oz) mushrooms, sliced

200 g (7 oz) can sweetcorn, drained

salt and pepper

1 tablespoons chopped chives, to garnish

Serves 4
Preparation time: 10 minutes
Cooking time: 30–35 minutes

sunshine citrus croissants

1 Place the croissants on a baking sheet and bake in a preheated oven, 190°C (375°F) Gas Mark 5, for about 5 minutes, until thoroughly heated and slightly toasted.

2 Meanwhile, grate the rind from the orange and stir it into the soured cream. Cut all the peel and white pith from the orange and grape-fruit, and carefully remove the segments with a sharp knife. Mix the segments with the cinnamon and sugar in a small saucepan. Heat gently for about 1–2 minutes.

3 Split the croissants lengthways and spoon the fruit mixture over the bottom halves. Top with a spoonful of the soured cream mixture, and replace the top halves. Serve warm.

4 croissants

1 orange

50 ml (2 fl oz) soured cream

1 small ruby or pink grapefruit

1 teaspoon ground cinnamon

1 tablespoon sugar

Makes 4

Preparation time: 15 minutes

Cooking time: about 5 minutes

pick up potatoes with creamy dip

1 If using wooden skewers, soak them in cold water for about 30 minutes to prevent burning.

2 Place the whole potatoes in a large pan of cold water, bring to the boil, reduce the heat and simmer for 15–20 minutes or until just tender. Drain, and when cool enough to handle, cut each potato into large wedges.

3 To make the creamy dip, place the garlic and egg yolks in a liquidizer or food processor, add the lemon juice and process briefly to mix. With the motor running, gradually add the oil in a thin stream until the mix forms a thick cream. Scrape into a bowl and stir in the sun-dried tomatoes, season with pepper, adding more lemon juice if liked.

4 Brush the potato wedges with the oil, sprinkle with a little paprika and skewer or lay the potato wedges on a heated griddle pan and cook for 5–6 minutes, turning often until golden brown all over. Sprinkle with sea salt flakes and serve with the creamy dip.

4 large potatoes, unpeeled
4 tablespoons olive oil
paprika
salt sea flakes

Creamy Dip:
4–6 garlic cloves, crushed
2 egg yolks
2 tablespoons lemon juice, plus extra to taste
300 ml (½ pint) extra virgin olive oil
8 sun-dried tomato halves in oil, drained and finely chopped
pepper

Serves 4

Preparation time: 10–15 minutes

Cooking time: 20–25 minutes

fisherman's catch ●

one fish, two fish ●

sailor's corn pie ●

honey & orange chicken sticks ●

potato & bacon boats ●

sausage & mash ●

chicken snakes ●

cheesy chicken balls ●

cheeseburgers de luxe ●

turkey burgers with barbecue sauce ●

star ham flan ●

chicken in a blanket ●

chicken drumsticks ●

cheesy bacon melts ●

chicken pot pie ●

surf
& turf

fisherman's catch

1   Wash the fish steaks under cold water and pat them dry with kitchen paper. Put all the marinade ingredients in a bowl and mix well. Add the fish steaks to the marinade, turning them until they are thoroughly coated and glistening with oil. Cover the bowl and leave in a cool dry place for at least 1 hour.

2   Heat the olive oil in a large frying pan. Remove the fish steaks from the marinade and fry gently until they are cooked and golden brown on both sides, turning the fish once during cooking. Remove the steaks from the pan and keep warm.

3   Meanwhile, make the tomato sauce. Heat the olive oil in a pan and sauté the garlic until just golden. Add the tomatoes and cook over a moderate heat until the tomatoes are reduced to a thick pulp. Season to taste with salt and pepper. Pour the sauce over the fish and sprinkle with oregano sprigs and leaves.

4 x 150 g (5 oz) white fish steaks, such as monkfish

3 tablespoons olive oil

Marinade:

5 tablespoons olive oil

2 tablespoons lemon juice

1 tablespoon finely chopped parsley

Tomato Sauce:

2 tablespoons olive oil

4 garlic cloves, chopped

750 g (1½ lb) tomatoes, skinned and chopped

salt and pepper

oregano sprigs and leaves, to garnish

Serves 4

Preparation time: 20 minutes, plus marinating

Cooking time: 20 minutes

one fish, two fish

1 Place the cod in a saucepan, cover with water, add the bay leaf and poach gently for 10 minutes. Remove from the pan and discard the skin and any bones, then flake the flesh. Meanwhile, cook the potatoes in a saucepan of boiling salted water until tender. Drain well and mash with half the butter. Melt the remaining butter in a frying pan, add the onion and fry for 5 minutes until softened. In a bowl, beat together the fish, potato and onion and season to taste. Stir in half the beaten egg to bind. Set the fish mixture aside in a cool place for 15–20 minutes to firm up.

2 Divide the fish mixture into 8 portions and mould into fish shapes. Coat first with flour, then with the remaining beaten egg, then with breadcrumbs.

3 Heat the oil in a frying pan and add the fish cakes, a few at a time. Fry, turning occasionally, for 5–8 minutes, or until cooked through and golden. Drain on kitchen paper. Keep hot on a heated serving dish while frying the remaining fish cakes. Let the junior chefs arrange the lemon slices on the fish to represent fins, the tomato wedges for mouths and the peas as eyes. Serve with peas or mixed vegetables.

375 g (12 oz) cod fillet

1 bay leaf

2 medium potatoes

50 g (2 oz) butter or margarine

1 small onion, finely chopped

2 eggs, beaten

50 g (2 oz) plain flour

125 g (4 oz) fresh white breadcrumbs

vegetable oil, for frying

salt and pepper

To Garnish:

8 lemon slices

8 tomato wedges

8 cooked peas

Serves 4

Preparation time: 15 minutes plus chilling

Cooking time: 30–40 minutes

sailor's corn pie

1 Cook the potatoes in a saucepan of salted boiling water for about 20 minutes or until tender. Drain well, return to the pan and shake over a low heat to dry. Add 25 g (1 oz) of the butter or margarine, half the cheese and salt and pepper to taste. Mash well with a potato masher or fork.

2 Meanwhile, place the fish in a large saucepan, add the milk, cover and cook over a gentle heat for 7 minutes. Strain, reserving the milk in a measuring jug, and leave the fish to cool slightly. Flake the fish, discarding the skin and bones. Make up the reserved milk to 450 ml (¾ pint) with extra milk or water, if necessary.

3 Melt the remaining butter or margarine in a saucepan. Sprinkle in the flour and cook, stirring well, for 1 minute. Gradually add the measured liquid, stirring the sauce constantly until it boils and thickens. Remove the sauce from the heat and stir in the remaining cheese with the sweetcorn and flaked fish. Season to taste with salt and pepper and stir well to mix. Turn the mixture into a 1.2 litre (2 pint) ovenproof dish.

4 Cover the fish mixture with the mashed potato and make little waves with a butter knife. Cook in a preheated oven, 180°C (350°F) Gas Mark 4, for 35–40 minutes until the topping is golden brown and the pie is heated through. Serve hot.

1 kg (2 lb) potatoes, peeled and cut into even-sized pieces

65 g (2½ oz) butter or margarine

125 g (4 oz) Cheddar cheese, finely grated

500 g (1 lb) smoked haddock or smoked cod fillets

450 ml (¾ pint) milk

25 g (1 oz) plain flour

125 g (4 oz) drained canned or thawed frozen sweetcorn

salt and pepper

Serves 4–6

Preparation time: 20 minutes

Cooking time: about 1 hour

honey & orange chicken sticks

1 To make the marinade, place the ginger, garlic, orange rind and juice, oil and honey in a large bowl and mix together. Cut each chicken breast into 8 long thin strips and coat with the marinade. Cover and set aside to marinate for 1–2 hours. If using wooden skewers soak them in cold water for 30 minutes.

2 To make the salsa, brush the corn cobs with 2 tablespoons of the oil and place under a preheated grill. Cook for 10–15 minutes, turning frequently, until the cobs are charred and the kernels are tender. Remove from the heat and when cool enough to handle remove the kernels from the cobs with a sharp knife. (Alternatively, cook the cobs on the barbecue, then remove the kernels.)

3 Place the kernels in a bowl, add the remaining oil, spring onions, coriander, sesame seeds, lime juice, soy sauce and sesame oil and season to taste. Set aside.

4 Remove the chicken from the marinade and thread 2 pieces on to each skewer. Place the skewers under a preheated grill or on the barbecue grill and cook for 2–3 minutes on each side until cooked through, basting with any remaining marinade. Serve with the toasted sweetcorn salsa and a green salad.

4 x 175 g (6 oz) boneless, skinless chicken breasts

Sweetcorn Salsa:

2 corn cobs, husks and inner silks removed

3 tablespoons sunflower oil

4 spring onions, chopped

3 tablespoons chopped coriander

2 teaspoons toasted sesame seeds

1 tablespoon lime juice

1 tablespoon light soy sauce

1 teaspoon sesame oil

salt and pepper

Marinade:

2.5 cm (1 inch) piece of fresh root ginger, peeled and very finely grated

2 garlic cloves, crushed

finely grated rind and juice of 1 orange

2 tablespoons olive oil

2 tablespoons honey

Serves 4
Preparation time: 30 minutes, plus marinating
Cooking time: 12–18 minutes

potato & bacon boats

1 Scrub the potatoes well, and dry. Prick the skins with a fork, and place the potatoes in a roasting tin or directly on the shelf of a preheated oven, 220°C (425°F), Gas Mark 7, and cook for about 1–1½ hours.

2 When cooked and soft to the touch, remove from the oven and slice off the tops. Scoop out the soft potato and place in a bowl. Add the bacon, milk and salt and pepper; mix well and pile back into the skins.

3 Place the potatoes back in the oven and reheat gently for about 5 minutes.

4 Meanwhile, prepare the garnish. Pleat the remaining bacon slices and push on to a skewer. Grill until crisp. Top each potato with a bacon slice, parsley or chives and some soured cream.

■ If you prefer a soft skin, wrap the potatoes in foil before baking. For crisp skins, rub the skins with oil and a little salt before baking.

4 firm, even-sized potatoes

250 g (8 oz) streaky bacon, grilled until crisp, and chopped

4 tablespoons milk

salt and pepper

To Garnish:

4 rashers of streaky bacon

1 tablespoon chopped parsley or chopped chives

4 tablespoons soured cream

Serves 4
Preparation time: 20 minutes
Cooking time: 1–1½ hours

1 Grill the sausages under a preheated hot grill for about 8–10 minutes, turning, until golden brown. Drain on kitchen paper, then cut into chunks and put them in a flameproof casserole.

2 Arrange the tomatoes around the sausages, cut sides up. Mash the potatoes with the butter or margarine and milk in a large bowl, to give a very soft consistency. Season to taste with salt and pepper.

3 Whisk the egg whites in a grease-free bowl until stiff peaks form: fold lightly but thoroughly into the potato mixture. Spoon the potato mixture around the sausages and tomatoes. Bake in a preheated oven, 200°C (400°F), Gas Mark 6, for about 20 minutes or until well risen and golden. Serve immediately.

500 g (1 lb) pork sausages

6 tomatoes, skinned and halved

3 large potatoes, cooked

50 g (2 oz) butter or margarine

300 ml (½ pint) milk

3 egg whites

salt and pepper

Serves 4

Preparation time: 20 minutes

Cooking time: 30 minutes

sausage & mash

chicken snakes

1 To make the marinade, combine the onion, garlic, sugar and soy sauce in a shallow dish. Add the chicken strips and stir well to coat. Cover and marinate for at least 1 hour.

2 To make the peanut sauce, put the peanuts in a liquidizer or food processor with the garlic and ginger, process until finely ground, then transfer to a saucepan and add the coconut milk, water, lime juice and sugar. Simmer over a moderate heat, stirring frequently, for 10–15 minutes or until the sauce is thick. Remove from the heat.

3 Thread the chicken strips on to the soaked bamboo skewers. Put the skewers on a hot griddle pan or the grid over hot charcoal on the barbecue. Cook, turning frequently, for 5–8 minutes until the chicken is charred on the outside and no longer pink on the inside.

4 Meanwhile, reheat the peanut sauce and transfer it to a serving bowl. Serve the snakes hot as a starter or snack, with the peanut sauce for dipping. Diced cucumber and rice are tasty accompaniments.

■ Soak wooden skewers for about 30 minutes before use on a grill to prevent them burning and catching alight.

4 large boneless, skinless chicken breast fillets, cut diagonally into thin strips

Marinade:

¼ onion, grated or chopped very finely

1 garlic clove, crushed

2 teaspoons soft brown sugar

2 tablespoons soy sauce

Peanut Sauce:

125 g (4 oz) dry roasted peanuts

2 garlic cloves, roughly chopped

2.5 cm (1 inch) piece fresh root ginger, roughly chopped

300 ml (½ pint) canned coconut milk

300 ml (½ pint) water

4 tablespoons lime juice

2 teaspoons soft brown sugar

Serves 4–6

Preparation time: about 30 minutes, plus marinating

Cooking time: about 30 minutes

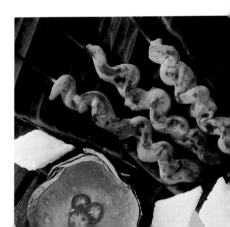

cheesy chicken balls

1 Melt the butter in a saucepan, add 25 g (1 oz) of the flour and cook for 1 minute, stirring. Gradually add the milk and bring to the boil, stirring until the sauce thickens. Remove from the heat and stir in the chicken, onion, Cheddar and parsley. Add salt and pepper to taste. Set aside to cool for 30 minutes.

2 Divide the mixture into 12 equal pieces and shape each one into a ball, using lightly floured hands. Roll each ball in the remaining flour, dip in beaten egg and coat in the breadcrumbs, pressing them on firmly.

3 Heat the oil in a deep fryer to 180–190°C (350–375°F) or until a cube of bread browns in 30 seconds. Add half the balls and fry for 6–7 minutes, turning, until golden brown and cooked through. Drain well on kitchen paper and keep warm while frying the remainder in the same way. Serve hot with chips or creamed potatoes and peas, or cold with salad.

25 g (1 oz) butter

40 g (1½ oz) plain flour

150 ml (¼ pint) milk

250 g (8 oz) cooked chicken, finely chopped

1 onion, finely chopped

75 g (3 oz) Cheddar cheese, grated

1 tablespoon chopped parsley

1 egg, beaten

50 g (2 oz) soft white breadcrumbs

vegetable oil, for deep frying

salt and pepper

Makes 12

Preparation time: 15 minutes, plus cooling

Cooking time: 20 minutes

cheeseburgers de luxe

1 Season the minced beef with salt and pepper, add the onion, if using, and form into 6 round flat cakes. If the meat is very lean, you may need to grease the grill pan or barbecue grill with a little oil. If there is a reasonable amount of fat in the meat, this is not necessary. The pan or grill should be preheated so that the meat starts to cook the moment it touches the surface.

2 Grill the hamburgers under a hot grill or over a barbecue for about 8–10 minutes, turning once. Alternatively, fry in a frying pan. Add the cheese slices a few minutes before the end of cooking time, so they melt slightly.

3 Serve the burgers in toasted hamburger buns with tomato ketchup or tomatoes and lettuce.

500 g (1 lb) best quality minced lean beef

1 small onion, finely chopped (optional)

a little oil, for frying

6 cheese slices

salt and pepper

To Serve:

6 hamburger buns

tomato ketchup or very finely chopped tomatoes

lettuce leaves

Serves 6

Preparation time: 10 minutes

Cooking time: 8–10 minutes

turkey burgers
with barbecue sauce

1 Place the minced turkey in a large bowl and add the onion and parsley. Mix together well and season. Shape into 12 burgers. Place on a baking sheet and set aside.

2 To make the sauce, melt the butter in a pan over a moderate heat. Cook the onion and garlic until pale golden. Add the pepper and continue cooking for 5 minutes. Add the mushrooms, tomatoes and oregano and cook for 5–10 minutes.

3 Brush the burgers with a little sunflower oil if necessary and cook under a preheated moderate grill for about 7 minutes on each side until cooked. Serve immediately,with the sauce separately. Serve with rolls or baps and a selection of salads for a summer lunch or barbecue.

1 kg (2 lb) turkey meat, minced

1 onion, finely chopped

1 teaspoon chopped parsley

sunflower oil, for brushing

salt and pepper

rolls or wholemeal baps, to serve

Barbecue Sauce:

25 g (1 oz) butter

1 medium onion, finely sliced

2 garlic cloves, crushed

1 green pepper, cored, deseeded and sliced

125 g (4 oz) mushrooms, sliced

400 g (13 oz) can chopped tomatoes

2 teaspoons dried oregano

salt and pepper

Makes 12

Preparation time: 15 minutes

Cooking time: 35 minutes

star
ham flan

1. Mix together the flour and oatmeal in a bowl. Add the butter and rub it in with the fingertips until the mixture resembles fine breadcrumbs. Add 3–4 tablespoons of cold water and mix to a firm dough.

2. Knead briefly on a lightly floured surface, then roll out and line a 20 cm (8 inch) flan tin. Line with some crumpled foil and bake in a preheated oven, 200°C (400°F), Gas Mark 6, for 10 minutes. Remove the flan case from the oven and reduce the oven temperature to 180°C (350°F), Gas Mark 4.

3. Add the chicory to a saucepan of boiling water with the lemon juice. Cover the pan and cook for 10 minutes, until the chicory is just tender then drain well.

4. Cut each chicory head in half lengthways and wrap each piece in a slice of ham. Arrange in the pastry case radiating from the centre. Beat together the eggs, cream, Parmesan and seasoning, then pour into the pastry case. Bake the flan for 25–30 minutes, until the filling is firm and golden brown. Serve warm.

125 g (4 oz) plain flour

50 g (2 oz) oatmeal

75 g (3 oz) butter, diced

Filling:

3 small heads chicory

2 tablespoons lemon juice

6 slices Parma ham or cooked ham

2 eggs

150 ml (¼ pint) single cream

25 g (1 oz) grated Parmesan cheese

salt and pepper

Serves 4–6
Preparation time: 20 minutes
Cooking time: 45–50 minutes

1 First make the red sauce. Purée the tomatoes in a liquidizer or food processor with 3 tablespoons boiling water, or rub through a sieve until smooth. Heat the oil in a saucepan and sauté the onions and garlic until soft but not coloured. Stir in the tomato mixture, the reserved tomato juice, tomato purée, coriander, vinegar and sugar. Cover and simmer for 10 minutes.

2 Heat the oil in a frying pan and shallow-fry the tortillas, one at a time, over a moderate heat for a few seconds until they become limp. Pat the tortillas with kitchen paper and spread each one with a little red sauce. Put some chicken strips in the centre of each one. Sprinkle some Cheddar and mozzarella on top, reserving a little, and the onion.

3 Roll up the tortillas and place in a buttered ovenproof dish. Pour over the remaining sauce and scatter with the rest of the cheese. Bake in a preheated oven, 190°C (375°F), Gas Mark 5, for 15–20 minutes. Serve with guacamole, if liked.

12 soft corn tortillas

6 boneless, skinless chicken breasts, cut into strips and cooked

250 g (8 oz) Cheddar cheese, grated

125 g (4 oz) mozzarella cheese, diced

1 small red onion, finely chopped

oil, for shallow-frying

Red Sauce:

400 g (13 oz) can chopped tomatoes, drained and juice reserved

4 tablespoons oil

2 onions, chopped

2 garlic cloves, crushed

3 tablespoons tomato purée

1 teaspoon ground coriander

1½ tablespoons wine vinegar

1 teaspoon sugar

Serves 4–6
Preparation time: 25 minutes
Cooking time: 30–35 minutes

chicken in a blanket

chicken drumsticks

1 Season the chicken lightly with salt and pepper. Spread the flour on one plate, the whisked egg whites on a second plate and the bread-crumbs on a third. Mix the herbs with the breadcrumbs.

2 Coat the chicken drumsticks first in the flour then in the whisked egg whites, and then in the breadcrumbs. Press the breadcrumbs on firmly so that they adhere.

3 Heat the oil in a large frying pan (preferably non-stick) until very hot but not smoking. Add the drum-sticks and fry over a moderate heat, turning frequently, for about 5 minutes until golden on all sides.

4 Transfer the drumsticks to a baking tray and place in a preheated oven, 190°C (375°F), Gas Mark 5, for 40 minutes or until the chicken feels tender when pierced with a skewer or fork. Turn the drum-sticks over from time to time to ensure that they brown evenly. Serve hot, with lemon wedges. Potatoes and a seasonal vegetable or salad would be good accompaniments.

8 chicken drumsticks, skinned

2 tablespoons plain flour

2 egg whites, whisked lightly

75 g (3 oz) fresh white breadcrumbs

2 tablespoons chopped herbs (e.g. parsley, chives, tarragon)

2 tablespoons groundnut oil

salt and pepper

lemon wedges, to garnish

Serves 4
Preparation time: 15 minutes
Cooking time: about 45 minutes

These drumsticks are cooked in the oven without fat, making them a healthy alternative to fried chicken.

cheesy bacon melts

1 Melt 15 g (½ oz) of the butter in a saucepan, add the onion, mushrooms and bacon and cook over a gentle heat for 5 minutes. Stir in the flour and cook for 1 minute. Remove from the heat and gradually stir in the milk; return to the heat and bring to the boil, stirring. Lower the heat and cook for a further 2 minutes, stirring constantly. Add half of the grated Cheddar, stir, and keep hot.

2 Meanwhile, toast the crumpets lightly on both sides. Dice the remaining butter, mix with the tomato ketchup and spread gently over the crumpets. Spoon over the hot cheese mixture and arrange the tomato slices on top.

3 Sprinkle with the remaining cheese and cook under a preheated moderate grill until the topping is golden brown. Serve at once with a green salad.

65 g (2½ oz) butter

1 small onion, peeled and finely chopped

50 g (2 oz) button mushrooms, thinly sliced

50 g (2 oz) streaky bacon rashers, rinded and chopped

15 g (½ oz) plain flour

120 ml (4 fl oz) milk

75 g (3 oz) Cheddar cheese, grated

8 crumpets

1 tablespoon tomato ketchup

2 medium tomatoes, thinly sliced

Makes 8

Preparation time: 10 minutes

Cooking time: 15–20 minutes

■ If liked, substitute the bacon with chopped sausage or pepperoni slices and add a little chopped green pepper with the onion.

50

chicken pot pie

1 Heat the oil in a flameproof casserole. Sauté the chicken over a moderate heat for about 5 minutes until coloured on all sides. Remove and set aside on a plate.

2 Melt the butter in the casserole, then add the vegetables and toss in the oil and butter. Lower the heat, cover and sweat gently for 10 minutes. Sprinkle in the flour and mixed spice. Cook, stirring, for about 1–2 minutes, then gradually stir in the cider and stock. Bring to the boil, stirring, season to taste with salt and pepper, and add the chicken with any juices from the plate. Cover and cook gently for 10 minutes. Turn into a bowl and leave until cold.

3 Roll out the pastry on a lightly floured surface and cut out a lid to fit a 1 litre (2 pint) dish and a strip to go around the dish. From the trimmings, cut out pastry leaves or other fun shapes for the top of the pie. Spoon the cold mixture into the pie dish, putting a pie funnel in the centre. Brush the rim of the dish with water. Press the pastry strip into place, brush with water, and put the lid on top, cutting a hole for the pie funnel. Press the edges to seal, knock up and flute. Brush the pastry with beaten egg and stick the pastry leaves on top. Brush again with beaten egg.

4 Place in a preheated oven, 220°C (425°F), Gas Mark 7, for 30 minutes or until the pastry is crisp and golden. Serve hot with green vegetables.

2 tablespoons groundnut oil

12 boneless, skinless chicken thighs, cut into bite-sized pieces

15 g (½ oz) butter

375 g (12 oz) carrots, thickly sliced

375 g (12 oz) turnips or parsnips, thickly sliced

2 leeks, trimmed, cleaned and thickly sliced

2 tablespoons plain flour

½ teaspoon ground mixed spice

300 ml (½ pint) dry cider

150 ml (¼ pint) chicken stock

250 g (8 oz) puff pastry, thawed if frozen

beaten egg, to glaze

salt and pepper

Serve 4

Preparation time: 15 minutes, plus cooling

Cooking time: 1 hour

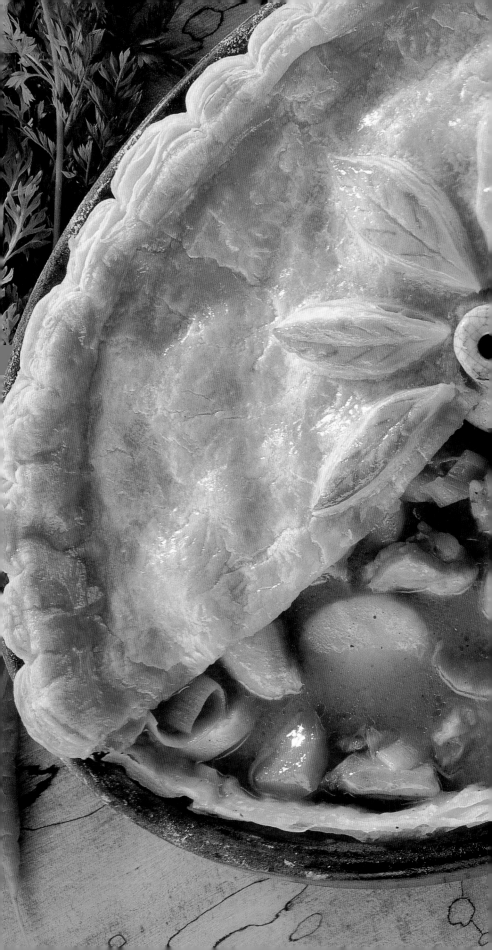

- magic bean bake
- macaroni cheese with ham
- coloured ribbon pasta
- stuffed vegetable pizza
- french bread pizzas
- bow tie pasta with chunky sauce
- mini pizzas
- lasagne surprise
- classic italian tagliatelle
- springy pasta salad

pasta
& pizza

magic bean bake

1 Pour the boiling water into a large, shallow, ovenproof dish and add the oil. Slide the sheets of lasagne into the dish and leave them for a few minutes to soften.

2 Put the broad beans into a saucepan of boiling water and cook for about 10 minutes, or until done. Drain well. Add the ratatouille and pepper to taste and heat through.

3 Remove the lasagne sheets and drain thoroughly, then spread them on a clean work surface. Divide the vegetable filling among the lasagne sheets, then roll them up to make cannelloni.

4 Place the rolled cannelloni in a shallow ovenproof dish and spoon over the chopped tomatoes. Cook in a preheated oven, 190°C (375°F), Gas Mark 5 for 30 minutes. To serve, sprinkle the cannelloni with the grated cheese and place under a preheated grill until just browned.

750 ml (1¼ pints) boiling water

½ teaspoon vegetable oil

8 sheets no pre-cook lasagne verde

125 g (4 oz) frozen broad beans

425 g (14 oz) can ratatouille

2 teaspoons chopped mixed herbs

400 g (13 oz) can chopped tomatoes

pepper

50 g (2 oz) Cheddar cheese, grated, to serve

Serves 4
Preparation time: 15 minutes
Cooking time: 45 minutes

■ Cover the cannelloni with foil and freeze for up to 3 months. Reheat from frozen in a moderate oven, 180°C (350°F), Gas Mark 4.

macaroni cheese with ham

1 Heat the butter and oil over a moderate heat. Add the garlic and ham, and fry gently for 4–5 minutes. Add the tomatoes and salt and pepper to taste. Simmer for 10–15 minutes or until well blended, stirring frequently.

2 Cook the macaroni in boiling salted water until just tender. Drain and toss with half the sauce. Transfer to a serving dish and spoon the remaining sauce over the top. Mix the basil with the cheese and sprinkle over the macaroni. Serve immediately.

40 g (1½ oz) butter

1 tablespoon olive oil

3 garlic cloves, finely chopped

175 g (6 oz) cooked ham, finely diced

400 g (13 oz) can chopped tomatoes

500 g (1 lb) macaroni

2 tablespoons chopped fresh basil

125 g (4 oz) freshly grated pecorino or Parmesan cheese

salt and pepper

Serves 6

Preparation time: 10 minutes

Cooking time: 30 minutes

coloured ribbon pasta

1 Heat half the oil in a pan and cook the garlic and onions for 8–10 minutes until soft and just beginning to colour. Add the pepper strips and cook until soft, then add the tomatoes and anchovies, if using, season with pepper and stir in the sugar. Cook for a few minutes longer until the tomatoes and anchovies are heated through.

2 Meanwhile, cook the trenette in boiling salted water for about 7 minutes until just tender. Drain well. Place in a hot serving dish and stir in a little sauce, half the cheese and, if liked, the remaining oil.

3 Pour over the rest of the sauce just before serving, and sprinkle the chopped parsley over the top. Serve the remaining grated cheese separately.

4–6 teaspoons olive oil

2 garlic cloves, crushed

2 large onions, finely chopped

1 red pepper, skinned, deseeded and cut into strips

400 g (13 oz) can chopped plum tomatoes

25 g (1 oz) can anchovy fillets in oil, drained (optional)

pinch of sugar

500 g (1 lb) trenette or other coloured pasta shapes

8 tablespoons grated Parmesan cheese

salt and pepper

1 tablespoon finely chopped parsley, to garnish

Serves 4

Preparation time: 15 minutes

Cooking time: 25 minutes

To remove the skin from a pepper, place the halved or quartered pepper under a moderately hot grill until the skin starts to blacken and curl. When cool enough to handle, peel off the skin with a sharp knife.

stuffed vegetable pizza

1 Blanch the mangetout, French beans and carrots in boiling salted water for 3 minutes. Drain and leave to cool. Cut the beans and mangetout in half and slice the artichokes. Mix all the vegetables together and set aside.

2 Melt the butter in a pan, add the flour and cook for 2 minutes, without browning. Gradually add the milk, bring to the boil, stirring, and cook for 2 minutes. Remove from the heat, stir in the cream, Parmesan, half of the Cheddar, the mixed herbs and egg yolks. Stir in all the vegetables.

3 Spoon the sauce into the centre of the pizza base and sprinkle over the remaining Cheddar. Slide the pizza on to a hot baking sheet and bake in a preheated oven, 200°C (400°F), Gas Mark 6, for 15–20 minutes (or according to packet instructions) until golden. Serve warm.

125 g (4 oz) mangetout

50 g (2 oz) French beans

50 g (2 oz) baby carrots, sliced

4 canned artichoke hearts, drained

25 g (1 oz) butter

25 g (1 oz) plain flour

150 ml (¼ pint) milk

2 tablespoons cream

25 g (1 oz) freshly grated Parmesan cheese

50 g (2 oz) mature Cheddar cheese, grated

pinch of dried mixed herbs

2 egg yolks

1 ready-made pizza base

salt and pepper

Makes 1 pizza

Preparation time: 10–15 minutes, plus standing

Cooking time: 20–25 minutes

■ Blanching means to boil food briefly in water. It is useful to blanch vegetables before freezing in order to retain colour, texture and flavour.

1 Slice the French stick in half lengthways and then in half crossways, on a slant. Place the bread under a preheated hot grill and toast the cut surfaces until golden.

2 Spread the cut surfaces with the tomato purée, then add the tomatoes, herbs, and the Cheddar. Arrange the anchovy fillets over the cheese on half the pizzas and the bacon on the rest. Garnish with olives.

3 Place the pizzas under a preheated moderate grill and cook for about 10 minutes until golden and bubbly. Serve hot.

1 large long French stick

3 tablespoons tomato purée

250 g (8 oz) can tomatoes, drained and chopped

1 teaspoon dried oregano or marjoram

125 g (4 oz) Cheddar cheese, grated

2 x 50 g (2 oz) cans anchovy fillets in oil, drained

125 g (4 oz) cooked bacon, crumbled

a few black and green olives, to garnish

Makes 4 French bread pizzas

Preparation time: 12 minutes

Cooking time: about 10 minutes

french bread pizzas

bow tie pasta with chunky sauce

1 Heat the oil in a large frying pan. Add the onion and garlic and fry for about 3 minutes until softened but not coloured.

2 Add the carrots and peppers and fry for a further 3 minutes. Stir in the wine with the chopped fresh tomatoes and canned tomatoes. Add salt and pepper to taste. Simmer, partially covered, for 15 minutes.

3 Meanwhile, bring 1.8 litres (3 pints) water to the boil in a large saucepan. Add a dash of oil and a generous pinch of salt. Cook the pasta for about 8–12 minutes, until just tender.

4 Drain the pasta, transfer it to a heated large serving platter, and season with black pepper. Drizzle with a little more oil if you wish. Pour over the sauce. Shred the basil leaves and scatter them over the sauce, then serve at once.

2 tablespoons olive oil

1 onion, chopped

2 garlic cloves, crushed

2 carrots, finely chopped

2 red peppers, cored, deseeded and finely chopped

150 ml (¼ pint) red wine

4 large tomatoes, chopped

400 g (13 oz) can chopped tomatoes with herbs

375 g (12 oz) dried farfalle (bow ties)

salt and pepper

1 bunch of basil, to garnish

Serves 4

Preparation time: 10 minutes

Cooking time: 20 minutes

mini pizzas

1 Divide the pizza dough into 4 pieces and roll out 4 x 12 cm (5 inch) circles, making the edges thicker, and place them on greased, perforated pizza pans. Brush each one with a little olive oil, then spread the tomato sauce evenly over the dough.

2 Place two-thirds of the pepperoni slices in the centre of one circle and top with 6 of the black olives and the capers. Sprinkle with the Parmesan. Shape the salami slices into cones and arrange them on the second dough circle. Top with the green olives.

3 Place the Gruyère slices and sun-dried tomato strips in the centre of the third circle, and arrange the remaining pepperoni slices around the edge. Arrange the mozzarella over the base of the fourth circle, then place the anchovies, if using, on top with the remaining black olive in the centre. Bake in a preheated oven, 200°C (400°F), Gas Mark 6, for about 15 minutes. Garnish with basil and serve hot.

ready-made pizza dough

olive oil, for brushing

175 ml (6 oz) ready-made tomato sauce

125 g (4 oz) pepperoni, thinly sliced

7 black olives, pitted and halved

1 teaspoon capers, drained

2 tablespoons freshly grated Parmesan cheese

6 slices salami

6–12 green olives, pitted

50 g (2 oz) Gruyère cheese, sliced

1 sun-dried tomato, cut into strips

50 g (2 oz) mozzarella cheese, sliced

6 anchovy fillets (optional)

chopped basil, to garnish

Makes 4 x 12 cm (5 inch) pizzas

Preparation time: 25 minutes

Cooking time: 15 minutes

lasagne surprise

1 In a bowl, mix the beef and ham with the onion, stir in the tomato purée and egg yolks and season to taste. Take heaped teaspoons of the mixture and shape into balls, using floured hands. Heat the oil in a large frying pan, add the meatballs and fry for about 5 minutes, turning occasionally, until evenly browned. Remove with a slotted spoon.

2 Add the lasagne one sheet at a time to a large saucepan of lightly salted boiling water and boil for 10–12 minutes, then drain well.

3 Meanwhile, make the sauce. Melt the butter in a saucepan, sprinkle in the flour and cook for 1–2 minutes, stirring constantly. Remove from the heat and gradually stir in the milk. Return to the heat and simmer for 2 minutes, stirring constantly until thickened and smooth. Stir in the mozzarella and season to taste.

4 Lay the lasagne sheets in a single layer on a wet tea towel, to prevent them from sticking together. Spoon a little of the sauce over the base of a greased, large, rectangular ovenproof dish. Add a layer of lasagne, a few meatballs, and a little more of the sauce. Continue with alternate layers of lasagne, meatballs and sauce, finishing with a layer of sauce. Sprinkle the top with the grated Parmesan. Cook in a preheated oven, 190°C (375°F), Gas Mark 5, for 35–40 minutes until golden. Serve hot.

375 g (12 oz) lean minced beef

175 g (6 oz) cooked ham, minced

1 small onion, grated

1 teaspoon tomato purée

3 egg yolks

vegetable oil, for frying

250 g (8 oz) lasagne sheets

salt and pepper

Sauce:

50 g (2 oz) butter

50 g (2 oz) plain flour

750 ml (1¼ pints) milk

175 g (6 oz) mozzarella cheese, diced

4 tablespoons grated Parmesan cheese

Serves 6

Preparation time: 25 minutes

Cooking time: about 1 hour

classic italian tagliatelle

1 Heat 3 tablespoons of the olive oil in a large frying pan. Add the onions and garlic, and sauté gently over low heat for about 5–8 minutes until they are tender and slightly coloured. Stir the mixture occasionally.

2 Add the tomatoes and tomato purée together with the sugar and wine, stirring well. Cook over a gentle heat until the mixture is quite thick and reduced. Stir in the quartered olives and torn basil leaves and season to taste with salt and pepper.

3 Meanwhile, add the tagliatelle to a large pan of boiling salted water (to which a little oil has been added to prevent the pasta sticking). Boil rapidly until the tagliatelle is just tender but still firm (al dente). Drain the tagliatelle immediately, mixing in the remaining olive oil and a grinding of pepper. Arrange the pasta on 4 serving plates and top with the tomato sauce, mixing it into the tagliatelle. Serve sprinkled with Parmesan.

4 tablespoons olive oil

2 onions, chopped

2 garlic cloves, crushed

500 g (1 lb) plum tomatoes, skinned and chopped

2 tablespoons tomato purée

1 teaspoon sugar

100 ml (3½ fl oz) dry white wine

a few olives, pitted and quartered

a handful of torn basil leaves

375 g (12 oz) dried tagliatelle

50 g (2 oz) grated Parmesan cheese

salt and pepper

Serves 4

Preparation time: 10 minutes

Cooking time: 20–25 minutes

springy pasta salad

1 Bring a large pan of salted water to the boil. Add the pasta and cook for 12–15 minutes. Drain and rinse under cold water. At the same time cook the sweetcorn according to the packet instructions. Leave the cooked and drained pasta and sweet-corn to cool slightly. Combine them with the celery, tomatoes and spring onions in a large mixing bowl.

2 Blend the dressing ingredients together in a small bowl and season. Pour the dressing over the salad and toss lightly. Spoon the salad into a serving dish and sprinkle with parsley. Cover and chill slightly before serving, garnished with parsley and celery leaves.

125 g (4 oz) pasta twists or shells

175 g (6 oz) frozen sweetcorn

4 celery sticks, washed and sliced

4 tomatoes, skinned, quartered and deseeded

4 spring onions, chopped

salt and pepper

To Garnish:

chopped parsley

celery leaves

Dressing:

150 g (5 oz) natural low-fat yogurt

4 tablespoons tomato juice

½ teaspoon Worcestershire sauce

pinch of sugar

Serves 6

Preparation time: 20 minutes plus chilling

Cooking time: 15 minutes

- fruit fondue
- madeleine castles
- banana lollies
- cranberry tart
- pink pudding in a cloud
- watermelon ice
- monkey's favourite cake
- chocolate cinnamon crunchies
- oat & raisin cookies
- victoria sandwich
- apple sauce cake
- gingerbread cookies
- crazy cupcakes
- chocolate crispy treats

yummy treats

fruit fondue

1 Break all of the chocolate into a heatproof bowl and add the cream. Place over a saucepan of gently simmering water. Stir until the chocolate has melted.

2 Pour the sauce into a warmed heatproof bowl. Serve with a selection of fresh fruit and biscuits for dipping, using cocktail sticks to spear the fruit.

■ If serving this dish to small children, it is best to omit the the cocktail sticks and just let little eaters use their fingers!

50 g (2 oz) milk chocolate

25 g (2 oz) plain chocolate

1 tablespoon double cream

To Serve:

selection of fruit, including cherries, strawberries, raspberries, sliced banana

sponge fingers or langues de chat

20 minutes

Cooking time: 10 minutes

madeleine castles

1. Sieve the flour with a pinch of salt in a bowl. In another bowl, cream the butter and sugar until light and fluffy, then beat in the eggs, one at a time. Fold in the flour to the butter mixture and mix well.

2. Half fill 18 well greased dariole tins. Bake in a preheated oven, 220°C (425°F), Gas Mark 7, for about 12 minutes, or until firm and golden brown. Remove from the tins and cool on a wire rack.

3. Heat the jam gently and beat out any whole pieces of fruit. Insert a fork into the base of the cakes and spread the jam over the sides and top. Put the coconut on to a sheet of greeseproof paper and roll cakes in it, covering well. Remove the fork.

4. Decorate each cake with a glacé cherry.

125 g (4 oz) self-raising flour
125 g (4 oz) butter or margarine
125 g (4 oz) caster sugar
2 eggs, lightly beaten
6 tablespoons raspberry jam
desiccated coconut, to cover
glacé cherry halves, to decorate
salt

Makes 18
Preparation time: 20 minutes, plus cooling
Cooking time: about 12 minutes

banana lollies

1 Cut each banana in half cross-ways. Fix each banana half on to a wooden skewer so that the skewer penetrates at least 5 cm (2 inches) into the banana. Place the bananas on a sheet of foil and chill in the freezer for 1 hour.

2 Place the chocolate and butter in a heatproof bowl set over a saucepan of simmering water. Stir until the chocolate has melted. Remove one banana half at a time from the freezer, hold it over the bowl and spoon the melted chocolate over the banana to coat well. The chocolate coating will begin to set immediately on the bananas.

3 Sprinkle the chocolate-coated bananas with hundreds and thousands and lay them carefully on a sheet of lightly oiled greaseproof paper, or push the sticks into a block of flower-arranging oasis. Leave to set completely, then wrap lightly in foil or freezer wrap, and return to the freezer. Serve the lollies ice-cold, straight from the freezer.

6 large firm bananas, peeled

12 wooden skewers or thin lolly sticks

375 g (12 oz) plain or milk chocolate, broken into pieces

15 g (½ oz) butter

coloured hundreds and thousands or chocolate vermicelli, to decorate

Makes 12

Preparation time: 15 minutes plus freezing

cranberry tart

1 Place the flour in a bowl, add the diced butter and rub it in with the fingertips until the mixture resembles fine breadcrumbs. Stir in the caster sugar and grated orange rind, then add the beaten egg and enough water to mix to a soft dough.

2 Turn out the dough on to a lightly floured surface and knead briefly. Roll out and use to line a 25 x 15 cm (10 x 6 inch) shallow rectangular tin. Trim the edges, reserving the trimmings.

3 Stir the cranberries into the mincemeat and spread the mixture over the base of the pastry case. Reroll the reserved pastry trimmings and use a cutter to cut into small stars or holly shapes. Arrange the shapes over the mincemeat mixture.

4 Brush the pastry with milk and sprinkle with a little sugar. Bake in a preheated oven, 190°C (375°F), Gas Mark 5, for 25–30 minutes until the pastry is golden brown. Sprinkle with caster sugar. Cut the tart into 6 squares and serve warm with some whipped cream or warm pouring custard, if liked.

250 g (8 oz) self-raising flour

125 g (4 oz) chilled butter, diced

75 g (3 oz) caster sugar

grated rind of 1 orange

1 egg, beaten

milk, to glaze

caster sugar, for sprinkling

Filling:

250 g (8 oz) fresh or frozen cranberries, thawed

250 g (8 oz) mincemeat

Serves 6
Preparation time: 20 minutes
Cooking time: 25–30 minutes

1 Set aside 6 raspberries to use for decoration. Place the remainder in a liquidizer or food processor with the sugar and work to a purée. Rub through a sieve to remove the pips.

2 Fold the purée into the cream, then spoon into 6 individual glasses, cover and chill until set. Decorate each one with a raspberry and serve with sweet biscuits, if liked.

300 g (10 oz) raspberries

75 g (3 oz) caster sugar

300 ml (½ pint) whipping cream, whipped

Serves 6

Preparation time: 10 minutes, plus chilling

pink pudding in a cloud

watermelon ice

1 Discard the seeds and scoop out the flesh from the watermelon, reserving the shell. Cut the shell into 4 wedges. Place in a freezerproof bowl of matching size and reshape. Chill.

2 Place the flesh from the water-melon in a liquidizer or food processor with the sugar and lemon juice. Blend until smooth. Pour into a freezerproof container and freeze for 3–4 hours. Spoon into a chilled bowl and whisk until fluffy.

3 Turn the half-frozen mixture into the watermelon shell and smooth the top. Cover with foil and freeze until solid. About 10 minutes before serving, remove the melon wedges from the freezer and separate them with a warmed knife. Decorate with mint sprigs and serve at once.

½ small watermelon, weighing about 1.25 kg (2½ lb)

125 g (4 oz) icing sugar, sifted

8 tablespoons lemon juice

mint sprigs, to decorate

Serves 4

Preparation time: 15 minutes, plus freezing

monkey's favourite cake

1 Line and grease two 18 cm (7 inch) sandwich tins.

2 Cream the butter and sugar together until pale and fluffy. Add the eggs, one at a time, adding a tablespoon of flour with the second egg. Fold in the remaining flour with the bananas.

3 Divide the mixture between the prepared sandwich tins. Bake in a preheated oven, 180°C (350°F), Gas Mark 4, for 20–25 minutes until the cakes spring back when lightly pressed. Turn out the cakes on to a wire rack to cool.

4 To make the filling, mix the ground almonds with the icing sugar, then add the banana and lemon juice and mix to a smooth paste. Sandwich the cakes together with the filling and dust with icing sugar.

125 g (4 oz) butter or margarine

125 g (4 oz) caster sugar

2 eggs

125 g (4 oz) self-raising flour, sifted

2 bananas, mashed

icing sugar, for dusting

Filling:

50 g (2 oz) ground almonds

50 g (2 oz) icing sugar, sifted

1 small banana, mashed

½ teaspoon lemon juice

Makes one 18 cm (7 inch) cake
Preparation time: 15 minutes
Cooking time: 20–25 minutes

chocolate cinnamon crunchies

1 Sift the flour, bicarbonate of soda, cinnamon and salt into a bowl, then set aside.

2 In a large bowl, beat together the butter and cooking fat. Add 225 g (7½ oz) of the sugar and beat until fluffy. Add the vanilla, then the egg, beating well. Blend in the syrup and chocolate. Gradually work in the flour mixture, beating until combined.

3 Spread the remaining sugar in a shallow tin. Shape the dough into balls about 3½ cm (1½ inches) in diameter. Place the balls, 6–8 at a time in the tin and roll in the sugar to coat them lightly all over. Place the balls about 5 cm (2 inches) apart on ungreased baking sheets.

4 Bake in preheated oven, 180°C (350°F), Gas Mark 4, for about 15 minutes or until the cookies feel firm when touched lightly. Leave the cookies on the baking sheets for about 2 minutes, then transfer to wire racks to cool completely.

250 g (8 oz) plain flour

2 teaspoons bicarbonate of soda

1 teaspoon ground cinnamon

¼ teaspoon salt

125 g (4 oz) butter, softened

50 g (2 oz) vegetable cooking fat

275 g (9 oz) sugar

½ teaspoon vanilla essence

1 egg

3 tablespoons golden syrup

50 g (2 oz) plain chocolate, melted and cooled

Makes about 25

Preparation time: 20 minutes

Cooking time: 15 minutes

oat & raisin cookies

1 Cover the raisins with the hot water and set aside to soak for 15 minutes. Drain well and reserve 50 ml (2 fl oz) of the soaking liquid.

2 Beat the butter and sugar until pale and fluffy. Stir in the egg, vanilla essence and the raisins. Sift the flour, salt, bicarbonate of soda and cinnamon over the mixture. Stir well, adding the reserved water and oats, to make a soft dough. Using a dessert-spoon, place balls, well apart, on greased baking sheets. Flatten slightly with a fork. Bake in a preheated oven 190°C (375°F), Gas Mark 5, for about 15–20 minutes. Leave for 2 minutes, then transfer to a wire rack to cool.

90 g (3½ oz) raisins

125 ml (4 fl oz) hot water

175 g (6 oz) butter

175 g (6 oz) soft light brown sugar

1 egg, beaten

1 teaspoon vanilla essence

125 g (4 oz) plain flour

1 teaspoon salt

½ teaspoon bicarbonate of soda

½ teaspoon cinnamon

250 g (8 oz) rolled oats

Makes about 25

Preparation time: 15 minutes plus soaking

Cooking time: 15–20 minutes

victoria sandwich

1 Line and grease two 18 cm (7 inch) sandwich tins.

2 Cream the butter and sugar together until pale and fluffy. Beat in the eggs, one at a time, adding a tablespoon of the flour with the second egg. Fold in the rest of the flour, then the water.

3 Divide the mixture between the prepared tins and bake in a preheated oven, 190°C (375°F), Gas Mark 5, for 20–25 minutes, until the cakes are golden, and spring back when lightly pressed. Turn on to a wire rack to cool. Sandwich the cakes together with the cream and jam and sprinkle the top with icing sugar.

■ To make a decorative pattern, place a paper doily on the cake and then gently sprinkle over the sugar.

125 g (4 oz) butter or margarine

125 g (4 oz) caster sugar

2 eggs

125 g (4 oz) self-raising flour, sifted

1 tablespoon hot water

To Decorate:

150 ml (¼ pint) double cream, lightly whipped

3 tablespoons jam

icing sugar

Makes one 18 cm (7 inch) cake
Preparation time: 15 minutes
Cooking time: 20–25 minutes

apple sauce cake

1 Soak the raisins in enough hot water to cover them for about 15 minutes, then drain, discarding the soaking water.

2 Sift the flour, bicarbonate of soda and spices together and set aside. Beat the butter with the brown sugar until light and fluffy. Beat in the egg and vanilla, then stir in the apple sauce, chopped nuts and drained raisins. Add the flour mixture to the creamed mixture in three batches, folding well to combine after each addition.

3 Pour the cake into a well-greased 23 cm (9 inch square) or 18 x 28 cm (7 x 11 inch) rectangular cake tin. Bake in a preheated oven, 180°C (350°F), Gas Mark 4, for about 50 minutes, or until a skewer inserted in the centre comes out clean. Cool in the baking tin on a wire rack.

4 Beat all the frosting ingredients together until smooth and well blended. Spread the frosting over the top of the cooled cake. Decorate with chopped walnuts or pecans and cut into squares to serve.

250 g (8 oz) raisins

300 g (10 oz) plain flour

2 teaspoons bicarbonate of soda

½ teaspoon ground nutmeg

¼ teaspoon ground cloves

½ teaspoon ground cinnamon

110 g (4 oz) butter

50 g (2 oz) soft brown sugar

1 egg

½ teaspoon vanilla essence

375 g (12 oz) unsweetened apple sauce

150 g (5 oz) chopped walnuts or pecans

chopped walnuts or pecans, to decorate (optional)

Frosting:

250 g (8 oz) cream cheese, softened

50 g (2 oz) dark brown sugar

¼ teaspoon grated orange rind

¼ teaspoon vanilla essence

2 teaspoons single cream or milk

Makes 9 squares

Preparation time: 25 minutes plus soaking

Cooking time: 50 minutes

1 Lightly grease a baking sheet.
   Sift the flour and ginger into a
bowl together. In another bowl, cream
the butter with the sugar until light
and fluffy.

2 Add the flour mixture and the
   treacle, mix, and then knead
until smooth.

3 Roll out the dough on a lightly
   floured surface to a thickness of
5 mm (¼ inch). Cut out gingerbread
people. Press in raisins for eyes and a
row of buttons. Use candied fruit peel
for the mouth. Place on the prepared
baking sheet and bake in a preheated
oven 190°C (375°F), Gas Mark 5, for 20
minutes. Allow to cool before serving.

300 g (10 oz) plain flour

1 teaspoon ground ginger

125 g (4 oz) butter or margarine

150 g (5 oz) dark brown sugar

50 ml (2 fl oz) treacle

To Decorate:

raisins

candied fruit peel

Makes 6
Preparation time: 10–15 minutes
Cooking time: 20 minutes

gingerbread cookies

crazy cupcakes

1 Stand 20 paper cake cases on a baking sheet.

2 Sift the flour into a mixing bowl. Add the margarine, sugar, eggs and vanilla essence, then beat with a wooden spoon for 1–2 minutes, until evenly blended.

3 Using a teaspoon, divide the mixture equally among the paper cases. Bake in a preheated oven, 180°C (375°F), Gas Mark 4, for about 15 minutes until golden and springy to the touch. Transfer the cakes in their cases to a wire rack and leave to cool completely.

4 To make the icing, sift the icing sugar into a bowl and mix in enough water to make a smooth coating consistency. Divide the icing into 3–4 portions, if liked, and colour each with different food colouring. Spread the icing over the tops of the cakes, decorate while the icing is still soft, then leave until the icing is set.

150 g (5 oz) self-raising flour

125 g (4 oz) soft margarine

125 g (4 oz) caster sugar

2 eggs

2–3 drops vanilla essence

Icing:

250 g (8 oz) icing sugar

2–3 tablespoons warm water

few drops of food colouring (optional)

To Decorate:

glacé cherries, hundreds and thousands, orange and lemon slices, chocolate vermicelli, tiny sweets

Makes 20
Preparation time: 15–20 minutes
Cooking time: 15 minutes

chocolate crispy treats

1 Line a 15 cm (6 inch) square cake tin with greaseproof paper. Put the marshmallows in a saucepan with the milk and heat very gently until the marshmallows have melted. (Stir well do the ingredients don't stick to the pan.)

2 Remove from the heat and stir in the Rice Krispies until well coated in the marshmallow mixture. Turn into the prepared tin.

3 Pack the mixture into an even layer and leave to cool for about 2 hours until set.

4 Remove from the tin and cut into squares. Gently melt the chocolate and drizzle over the cakes using a teaspoon or piping bag.

150 g (5 oz) marshmallows

3 tablespoons milk

100 g (3½ oz) Rice Krispies

25 g (1 oz) plain or milk chocolate

Makes 12	
Preparation time: 10 minutes, plus cooling	
Cooking time: 2 minutes	

■ Alternatively, omit the marshmallows and melt 150 g (5 oz) chocolate in the milk and continue as above. If you don't have a 15 cm (6 inch) tin, use a larger tin for thinner treats or a round tin.

cranberry smoothie ●

frosty lime-ade ●

mary poppins punch ●

very berry shake ●

chocolate shake ●

raspberry razzle ●

hot blackcurrant punch ●

bugs bunny juice ●

mocktails

cranberry smoothie

1 Put the cranberries, sugar, and water into a saucepan and heat gently to dissolve the sugar. Bring to the boil and cook for 5 minutes. Remove the pan from the heat and allow to cool completely.

2 Put the cranberry syrup in a liquidizer or food processor with the yogurt and coconut milk and blend until smooth. Divide the smoothie among four tall glasses filled with cracked ice cubes and serve each decorated with a sprig of mint, a cape gooseberry and a fresh cranberry threaded on to a cocktail stick.

■ This quick and easy healthy drink can be made with other fruits such as blueberries or cherries.

250 g (8 oz) cranberries, defrosted, if frozen

3 tablespoons sugar

125 ml (4 fl oz) water

450 ml (¾ pint) plain yogurt

250 ml (8 fl oz) coconut milk

To Serve:

cracked ice cubes

mint sprigs

cape gooseberries

fresh cranberries

Serves 4
Preparation time: 10 minutes, plus cooling
Cooking time: 5 minutes

1 scoop lime sorbet

4 teaspoons grapefruit juice

4 teaspoons mint syrup

1 Place the sorbet, grapefruit juice and mint syrup in a liquidizer or food processor and blend at high speed for about 30 seconds. Strain into a plastic cocktail glass or tumbler and decorate with fresh mint. Cut a small slit in the lemon slice and fix on to the rim of the glass.

To Decorate:

chopped mint

lemon slice

Serves 1
Preparation time: 5 minutes

frosty lime-ade

mary poppins punch

1   Freeze a large block of ice in a shallow container. Put the ice into a chilled punch bowl and pour over the ginger ale and lemonade. Stir and decorate with lemon slices, straws and paper parasols.

750 ml (1¼ pints) ginger ale

750 ml (1¼ pints) lemonade

lemon slices, to decorate

ice

Makes about 1.5 litres (2½ pints)

Preparation time: 5 minutes plus freezing

very berry shake

1 Put the crushed ice, strawberries, grenadine and cream into a liquidizer or food processor and blend on maximum speed for 30 seconds. Pour into a tumbler, add the dry ginger ale and stir.

2 Sprinkle a little ground ginger on top of the drink, if liked, and decorate with strawberries.

crushed ice

6–8 strawberries

40 ml (1½ fl oz) grenadine

40 ml (1½ fl oz) double cream

40 ml (1½ fl oz) dry ginger ale

pinch of ground ginger (optional)

whole strawberries, to decorate

Serves 1

Preparation time: 3 minutes

■ Grenadine is a sweet, red syrup that is used in drinks and desserts. Some variations contain alcohol, so be sure to check the label. It gets its name from Grenada, where it was originally made entirely from pomegranates.

chocolate shake

1 Pour all of the ingredients into a blender and blend until the desired thickness is reached. Pour into a glass and drink with a straw.

250 ml (8 fl oz) milk

2 scoops vanilla ice cream

1 scoop chocolate ice cream

50 ml (2 oz) chocolate syrup

Serves 1
Preparation time: 5 minutes

raspberry razzle

1 Put the sorbet, grenadine and lime juice into a liquidizer or food processor and blend until mushy. Pour into 2 tall glasses and add a scoop of vanilla ice cream to each. Top up with soda water. Stir gently and decorate with the fruit. Drink with a straw.

2 scoops raspberry sorbet

3 tablespoons grenadine

2 tablespoons lime juice

2 scoops vanilla ice cream

250 ml (8 fl oz) soda water

To Decorate:

slices of oranges, thinly chopped raspberries

Serves 2
Preparation time: 3 minutes

hot blackcurrant punch

1 Place the blackcurrant juice and orange juice in a large heatproof jug. Blend the cinnamon with a little of the boiling water, then add to the jug with sugar to taste. Float the orange slices on top. Serve in mugs.

Blackcurrants are very high in vitamin C, making this punch a good choice for the wintertime.

300 ml (½ pint) blackcurrant juice
300 ml (½ pint) orange juice
1 teaspoon ground cinnamon
2.5 litres (4 pints) boiling water
sugar, to taste
1 orange, thinly sliced

Makes 2.75 litres (4¾ pints)

Preparation time: 5 minutes

250 ml (8 fl oz) carrot juice

125 ml (4 fl oz) orange juice

300 ml (½ pint) single cream

crushed ice

thin slices of orange, to decorate

Serves 4

Preparation time: 5 minutes

1 Put the carrot juice, orange juice and cream into a cocktail shaker and shake well. Put the crushed ice into 4 tall glasses and pour the carrot drink on top. Decorate with slices of oranges and serve immediately.

bugs bunny juice

index

apples: apple sauce cake 82
  appletree salad 22
  hot apple muffins 21

bacon: cheesy bacon melts 49
  mini bacon & sausage rolls 15
  potato & bacon boats 38
banana lollies 71
beef: cheeseburgers de luxe 43
  lasagne surprise 63
biscuits 78–9, 83
blackcurrant punch 94
bow tie pasta with chunky sauce 61
broad beans: magic bean bake 54
Bugs Bunny juice 95

cakes 76, 80–2, 84
cannelloni: magic bean bake 54
cheese: cheese scones 18
  cheeseburgers de luxe 43
  cheesy bacon melts 49
  cheesy chicken balls 41
  cheesy waffles 12
  chicken in a blanket 46
  macaroni cheese with ham 56
  Parmesan cheese twists 24
chicken: cheesy chicken balls 41
  chicken drumsticks 48
  chicken in a blanket 46
  chicken pot pie 50
  chicken snakes 40
  honey & orange chicken sticks 36
chocolate: chocolate crispy treats 85
  chocolate shake 93
  cinnamon crunchies 78
cod: one fish, two fish 34
corn chowder 27
courgette fritters, sandy 16
cranberries: cranberry smoothie 88
  cranberry tart 72
crazy cupcakes 84
croissants, sunshine citrus 28
cucumber & strawberry salad 17

fish 32–5
fisherman's catch 32
flapjacks, nutty orange 20
fondue, fruit 68
French bread pizzas 60
fruit fondue 68

gingerbread cookies 83

ham flan, star 45

lasagne surprise 63
lime-ade, frosty 90
lollies, banana 71

macaroni cheese with ham 56
madeleine castles 70
magic bean bake 54
Mary Poppins punch 91

monkey's favourite cake 76
muffins, hot apple 21
mushroom sauce, potato cakes & 14

nutty orange flapjacks 20

oat & raisin cookies 79

Parmesan cheese twists 24
pasta salad, springy 65
pie, chicken pot 50
pink pudding in a cloud 74
pizzas: French bread pizzas 60
  mini pizzas 62
  stuffed vegetable pizza 58
potatoes: pick up potatoes with creamy dip 29
  potato & bacon boats 38
  potato cakes & mushroom sauce 14
  sailor's corn pie 35
  sausage & mash 39

raspberries: pink pudding in a cloud 74
  raspberry razzle 93
ribbon pasta, coloured 57

sailor's corn pie 35
salads 17, 22, 65
sandy courgette fritters 16
sausages: mini bacon & sausage rolls 15
  sausage & mash 39
scones, cheese 18
smoked haddock: sailor's corn pie 35
springy pasta salad 65
star ham flan 45
strawberries: cucumber & strawberry salad 17
  very berry shake 92
sunshine citrus croissants 28
sweetcorn: corn chowder 27

tagliatelle, classic Italian 64
tomatoes: bow tie pasta with chunky sauce 61
  classic Italian tagliatelle 64
traffic lights, toasted 23
tuna scramble rolls 26
turkey burgers with barbecue sauce 44

very berry shake 92
Victoria sandwich 80

waffles, cheesy 12
watermelon ice 75